Getting Business for Your Business Workbook

An Entrepreneur's Planning Diary

By L.A. Dyer

Copyright © 2018 L.A. Dyer

All rights reserved. No part of this book may be reproduced in any form or by any electronic or mechanical means, including information storage and retrieval systems, without permission in writing from the publisher and author, except by reviewers, who may quote brief passages in a review.

Cover design by L.A. Dyer

Visit http://www.LADyerbooks.com for more exciting products from this author.

ISBN: 9781730921933

DEDICATION

Special thanks to KDD, MJD, MAD, JLW-B, CB, TB, KB, SER, Shelly the Wonder Dog, and the rest of my family and friends who didn't laugh out loud (in front of me) when I told them what I was doing.

And JJW who said that writing was what was next for me.

To all the courageous entrepreneurs out there, don't let anything stop you. Ever.

CONTENTS

	Acknowledgments	i
1	**Write It Down**	1
2	**What's Your Business?**	3
3	**The Customer-Centered Marketing Message**	30
4	**Build Your Message**	39
5	**Building Your Brand with Marketing Communications**	52
6	**What's Next?**	82
	Appendix A: SBA Business Resources	98
	Appendix B: Business Development Overview: Promotional Strategy Based Around a Product	98

ACKNOWLEDGMENTS

Special thanks to Kevin Dyer for his excellent perspectives on business and Judith Braley for our weekly meetings.

Chapter 1

WRITE IT DOWN

"It had long since come to my attention that people of accomplishment rarely sat back and let things happen to them. They went out and happened to things." ...*Leonardo da Vinci (1452-1519)*

Well, you did it. You had an idea that bugged you (maybe for years) and you decided to turn it into a small business. Congratulations! You are going to be a success. You know how I know? Because you've got the heart to follow through and get it done.

So now that you have an idea for a business or just opened one up, what's next? How do you get business for your business? Well, that's what this handy workbook is all about.

In it you'll record your action items for:

- Defining what your business is
- Creating your business goals and the actions items to get those goals accomplished
- Developing your elevator pitch
- Creating your marketing communications
- Crafting your promotional strategy yourself, saving you time and money

Think of this as your business diary. The best way to get things into perspective is to write them down and that's why I put this book together. You can safely record all of your thoughts, ideas, dreams, and secrets about your new business. Sometimes it's hard to tell your friends, family, or colleagues about your business idea because you haven't got all of the details yet. This is a place where you can get everything out there without judgment, criticism, or confusing questions. A place where your business ideas come to life and you can see your business flourishing even before you make your first move.

I have been involved in some facet of business for over 30 years. First, working in civil engineering firms, then with Bell Labs and moving on to various startups and Fortune 500 companies. I have strategized for a number of different industries including telecom, construction, government, tax, senior care, and software. I have an MBA in marketing and a BFA in graphic design and have held the title of graphic designer, marketing communications strategist, and most recently business development manager. I have created numerous successful branding vehicles, including websites, brochures, business cards and email newsletters. I have read countless books on advertising, marketing, Social Media strategy, promotion, and business development. And now, I want to help you get business for your business by explaining how you can get it done for less money than you think.

Thank you for purchasing this workbook. It was a joy to write knowing that I could help you cash in with my knowledge. And if you like my book, please leave me a favorable review on Amazon, because like you, I'm trying to develop business for my business. And thank you in advance for doing that.

And if you haven't already, I encourage you to purchase the accompanying book for this workbook: *Getting Business for Your Business* on Amazon.

Now go forth and make money!

Chapter 2

WHAT'S YOUR BUSINESS?

Maybe you purchased this workbook and you already have an idea for a small business but haven't acted upon it yet. Or you just registered your business and you are wondering what's next. Or you want to be an entrepreneur and have so many ideas that you still need to work out the details. In this chapter, you will start making notes about your business ideas, dates, goals, actions, and yearly goal plans. At the end of this chapter you will have a better idea of what your business is.

Why should you do all of this? Well, you need a plan and that's what this book will help you produce. This workbook is where you will outline the future promotional activities to get business for your business. It's your ACTION PLAN!!! It describes how you are going to get customers, keep customers, and develop customers into partners.

<u>DO NOT AVOID DOING A PLAN!</u>

Let's begin.
Do you already have an idea for your product or service or are you just starting out and still brainstorming? Use the area below to list all of your business ideas.

_____

_____

_____

THE GETTING BUSINESS FOR YOUR BUSINESS WORKBOOK

Now let's drill down into some details:

Take one idea that you really love from what you wrote and pretend that your perfect business already exists and describe it fully below. Example: What's your business name? What are you selling? Who are selling to? Describe the inside of your store/office. Do you have employees? How many? Who's your customer? How much money do you make?

THE GETTING BUSINESS FOR YOUR BUSINESS WORKBOOK

To see if your business name is available, please see the following blog post at SBA.gov. **How to choose and claim your business name:** https://www.sba.gov/blogs/how-choose-claim-and-protect-your-business-name-online-and-offline

Business projected opening date: (When are you going to start selling your product or service?) _____

Why are you doing this? List your top five reasons for wanting to become an entrepreneur.

_____

_____

_____

_____

_____

_____

Did you know that you are more apt to accomplish you goals if you write them down? It is a proven truth. And when you write down the goal, list three actions that you will do to accomplish that goal. And if you really want to knock it out of the park - add some dates!

Business Goal #1: Example: *I'm going to find out how much it costs to make my product or I'm going to find out how I can start my service company.*

_____

_____

_____

List five actions you can take to accomplish that goal:

_____

_____

_____

_____

_____

_____

_____

_____

_____

_____

_____

_____

_____

Projected goal #1 completion date:

_____

Business Goal #2: Example: *I will have 15 customers in the first month.*

_____

_____

_____

List five actions you can take to accomplish Business Goal #2:

_____

_____

_____

_____

_____

_____

_____

_____

_____

_____

_____

_____

_____

_____

_____

Projected goal #2 completion date:

_____

Business Goal #3: Still another example would be that *I will be working out of my home or an office or a store front or some other location.*

_____

_____

_____

_____

_____

_____

_____

List five actions you can take to accomplish Business Goal #3:

_____

_____

_____

_____

_____

_____

_____

_____

_____

_____

_____

_____

_____

_____

_____

Projected goal #3 completion date:

_____

Now you have some immediate goals that you will act upon to get things going. Let's think from the end for a moment. Look at where you want your business to be in 6 months, one year, two years, and four years.

Okay, let's think about your six month plan.

How much profit do you want to have?

_____

If you have a product, how will you make that product? Will you hold inventory or does someone else do that? Describe the production of your product.

_____

_____

_____

_____

_____

Describe what you think your branding will look like.

Who are your suppliers?

If you have a service, how will you implement that service? Will you start at home? Do you go to the customer or do they come to you?

_____

_____

_____

_____

_____

_____

How will you promote that service? (Social Media, Tradeshows, Word-of-mouth, Advertising, etc.?) List a few ideas.

_____

_____

_____

_____

_____

How many customers do you want to have?

_____

How many long-term relationships will you develop? These can be with suppliers or other business colleagues as well as customers.

_____

_____

THE GETTING BUSINESS FOR YOUR BUSINESS WORKBOOK

List some ways you might accomplish this:

_____

_____

_____

_____

_____

_____

What major expenses will you have? Where are you getting the money to pay them?

_____

_____

_____

Thoughts on your sales strategy? (low price, technological, what makes you different?)

_____

_____

_____

_____

_____

_____

How will you promote your product? Advertising/Social Media/website/tradeshows/home parties?

_____

_____

_____

_____

_____

_____

_____

_____

Now, do the same thing for one, two, and four years. Keep checking and updating this list and change it as needed. This will help you determine the tactics (activities) you will need to undertake to accomplish your daily, monthly, and yearly goals. I also include this because it's your vision that will make this business successful. If you have an idea of where you are going, you'll know if you are getting off track and detailing these goals will also provide a better way to plan your money, time, and effort. You can find the one, two, and four year goal update sections at the back of this book.

Write down all your ideas around the following topics in your plan:

Develop your elevator pitch. If you were going to persuade an investor to invest in your company/product/service and you only had one minute to do it, how would you persuade them? Pretend you are charging yourself $100 per word and write out your elevator pitch. Pitch it to friends and family and see if they would invest!

_____

How do you think your product or service is different from your competitors?

Why should people purchase from you?

THE GETTING BUSINESS FOR YOUR BUSINESS WORKBOOK

_____

_____

_____

How many competitors are there? List them.

_____

_____

_____

_____

_____

_____

_____

Check your local library! Many public libraries have excellent business research resources. I prefer to research competitors on Hoovers Online and Mergent. It's great for customer or competitor research and includes sample business plans! Check your local library for details.

Your competitors:
       How much money do they make? _____
       How many customers do they have? _____
       What's makes them different from you?

_____

_____

_____

How are they the same?

_____

_____

_____

_____

Ideas to implement right now! Read the reviews of your competitors. Focus on the bad ones and make sure you DON'T do these things. Bad reviews are a great way to differentiate yourself from your competitor. Read your competitor reviews and write out in the following section how you would present your service or product differently. But remember, keep the name of your competitor out of the description. When you insult your competitor, you insult your potential customer who may have used that competitor.

_____

_____

_____

_____

_____

_____

_____

_____

_____

_____

_____

_____

_____

_____

What is the current economy? Good/bad? How does that determine how your product or service will be perceived?

_____

_____

_____

_____

_____

_____

What is the current state of your industry? What changes are you seeing? What problems need to be solved?

_____

_____

_____

_____

_____

_____

_____

_____

Your customers want what's original. And guess what? That's you! The perception of your business really boils down to who you are. So bring your thoughts, talents, sense of humor and caring for the customer. What a customer feels about your product or service has a direct impact on your sales, so put your uniqueness all over your business and your sales will benefit.

First, some by-the-book marketing information with the fours Ps of marketing:

Price: Where is your price in terms of the market and your competition? Are you at the bottom, top, middle? What price point will the market (your customers) pay with the least amount of resistance? Do you offer coupons, discounts, or promo codes? We'll get into this more when we discuss the benefits and value of your product or service in the next section.

Place: Where are you selling? Tradeshow, brick and mortar store, online, through a distribution network, out of your home?

Product: (Your service is also your product) What are the functions of your product or service? What's the packaging? (Describe the branding that you think will suit your product or service)

_____

_____

_____

_____

_____

_____

_____

_____

_____

_____

Promotion: How are you going to advertise/promote? All marketing communications would fall under "promotion" like brochures, websites, logos, stationary, and pretty much any messaging that goes out to your customer.

_____

_____

_____

_____

What are the strengths of your product/service/you? For more information on a SWOT analysis (Strengths, Weaknesses, Opportunities, and Threats), see chapter 3 of *Getting Business for Your Business*.

_____

_____

_____

_____

_____

_____

_____

_____

_____

_____

_____

_____

What are the weaknesses of your product/service/you (Can you make improvements? Or is there some new technology that you aren't implementing?)

_____

_____

_____

_____

_____

_____

_____

_____

THE GETTING BUSINESS FOR YOUR BUSINESS WORKBOOK

_____

_____

_____

_____

_____

_____

What is the pricing strategy of your competitors?

_____

_____

_____

What are the strengths of your competitors?

_____

_____

_____

What are the threats of your competitors?

_____

_____

_____

_____

_____

_____

_____

_____

How will you price your product or service?

_____

_____

What is your pricing strategy?
When you think about this, do you have a different price points? For example, do you have differentiated level of pricing like a luxury line?

_____

_____

_____

_____

_____

_____

_____

Do you have any employees yet? When do you plan on hiring?
_____

_____

Do you have an office? In your home? Downtown? What's the rent?
_____

_____

_____

How do you see your customers reacting to your product or service? Excited? Inquisitive? This helps with your customer experience. Whether it's a point & click or it's someone coming into your store, or someone using your service by just speaking with you over phone, I would suggest thinking out the experience you would like them to have. This helps when you are running your business. List out what you want your customer experience to be.

_____

_____

_____

_____

_____

_____

_____

_____

How will your product or service be distributed? Web? Brick & mortar?

What CRM (Customer Relationship Management) software will you use?

Who will set it up? You? If not, research some companies.

Who will use it? How many users will you have?

What markets can you think of? Are there other people in a different group who might be interested in your product or service? Like moms, dads, kids, accountants, or anyone else in a group? If you pinpoint a group you can produce more effective, specific marketing strategies for those groups.

Chapter 3

THE CUSTOMER-CENTERED MARKETING MESSAGE

Let's go deeper based on what you wrote in the last chapter.

Describe your ideal customer. Where do they live? What do they do? Who are they?

_____

_____

_____

_____

_____

_____

_____

_____

_____

_____

THE GETTING BUSINESS FOR YOUR BUSINESS WORKBOOK

_____

_____

_____

_____

_____

_____

What problem is your product or service going to solve for them?

_____

_____

_____

_____

_____

_____

_____

_____

_____

_____

_____

Describe how your product or service is going to make them feel.

_____

_____

_____

_____

_____

_____

Features vs. Benefits

Your messaging about your product has to "connect" with your customer. Using the features of your product or service to describe the benefits to your customer is a way to do that.

Features are the specifics of your product or service. Benefits are how your product or service helps the customer.

Let's say I've just come up with the most amazing idea ever. I've designed and manufactured a custom foot polisher (sorry, it's all I could come up with while writing this and my feet happen to be dry and scaly at the moment).

The features of my custom foot polisher are as follows:

- Automatic shut off
- Comfortable in your hand
- Delivered quickly
- Rechargeable
- Cordless
- Includes a nail customizer too!

So here's how to use the features to describe the benefits for your customer:

- Get your feet smooth even in winter

- Perfect for that time between pedicures
- Makes your feet look smaller
- Turns off by itself so no fire hazard
- Saves you money on batteries
- Makes your socks fit better
- Never get a run in your hose again
- Make your feet look great in the summer without the salon trip

Notice that the word *your* is used many times. Focus your messaging on the customer by using the word you and your wherever it will be most effective.

The difference between features and benefits is that features are what the P/S is and benefits are how the P/S makes the life of your customer better. **Your perceived benefits to the customer also help determine the value and pricing of your product or service.**
These are the things you want to concentrate on in your marketing and sales strategy. Again, exactly how does your customer get a fuzzy, warm feeling from your product or service? Does it bring them security? Does it save them money? Does it make them feel smart?

Describe your product or service features:

_____

_____

_____

_____

_____

_____

_____

_____

_____

_____

_____

_____

_____

Create your product or service benefits that you will use to persuade your customer to buy.

_____

_____

_____

_____

_____

_____

_____

_____

_____

_____

_____

Describe the value of your product or service to customers. An example would be the cost verses benefits. It's a good value if it brings many benefits for the cost.

_____

_____

_____

_____

_____

_____

What benefits does your product or service offer that your competitor's don't?

_____

_____

_____

_____

_____

_____

How much do you think your customers will pay for the uniqueness and benefits of your product or service? What's the most they will pay? What's the least?

_____

_____

When first going to market do you want to offer free samples and what will they be?

_____

_____

_____

_____

_____

_____

_____

_____

Do you want to offer your product for free to a select group of high influencing customers? And what will you offer to them?

_____

_____

_____

_____

_____

_____

_____

_____

Do you want to offer a discount code for first time buyers? If you did, what percentage would it be, how long would you offer it, how would you offer it (email sign up, etc.), and how do you think it would affect your profit?

Chapter 4

BUILD YOUR MESSAGE

Before you have communication with your customers, you have to determine what you are going to say. The goal of your messaging is to persuade your customer to buy your product or service. Your messaging supports your objectives and strategy.

Write out your elevator pitch again (with edits if you need to):

_____

_____

_____

_____

_____

_____

_____

_____

_____

_____

_____

_____

Your messaging is an expansion of your elevator pitch. It's really what you would say or write to get your customers to buy.

Keywords

While crafting your messaging you need to list the keywords associated with your product or service. Keywords are specific, descriptive words that are used to help your customer find your business online and satisfy search engine optimization (SEO) requirements. You can go online to and input your product or service name into different keyword trackers to see what phrases or keywords come up the most in searches for your product or service. Search online for "Keywords" to see what the keywords would be for your service or product.

What keywords will your customers use to search for your product or service online? What search phrases will they use?

_____

_____

_____

_____

_____

_____

_____

_____

Create a list of persuasive words that you might use to sell your product or service.

_____

_____

_____

_____

_____

Craft your marketing message and story about your product or service using the persuasive words from above (call, get, sale, etc.) and incorporate as many keywords or search phrases into the paragraph as you can and use the information from your benefits and features.

First Draft.

_____

_____

_____

_____

_____

_____

_____

_____

_____

Second Draft. Read your first draft out loud and flush out what you just wrote by eliminating any un-needed words. Does it sell? Would you buy what you are describing?

THE GETTING BUSINESS FOR YOUR BUSINESS WORKBOOK

Third Draft. Take what you just wrote and read it out loud. How does it sound? Do you like the flow? Does it sound easy or when you read it are there places where it just doesn't sound right? In the area below, write out a third paragraph incorporating any edits based on reading it out loud.

THE GETTING BUSINESS FOR YOUR BUSINESS WORKBOOK

Picture your customer reading your brochure, website, or any other messaging. Now write down five persuasive bullet points you can take from your messaging paragraph above that you want your customers to read first.

_____

_____

So now that you have your messaging, let's move onto where you will use it.

Chapter 5

BUILDING YOUR BRAND WITH MARKETING COMMUNICATIONS

Marketing communications is the communication of your brand to your customers with media and messaging. Marketing communications are designed with your objectives and strategy in mind. Here is a list of some common marketing communications:

- Websites
- Brochures
- Newsletters/ Email Communications
- Direct mail
- Coupons
- Presentations
- Business cards
- Social Media
- Trade shows

TIP: All of your marketing communications should be similar in look and feel with consistent keyword infused messaging. Always include your logo, contact information, and website address on every piece of marketing that goes out the door. Remember, a similar look and feel helps your customer remember your brand.

Your logo.
Your logo should be very simple because intricate logos can be a nightmare to print. If you look at various small business', you will see that most logos are very simple. Also, think about your small logo on a business card. Will it look okay that small?

Sketch out your logo idea:

You can design a logo in Word or there are many online logo designers available – some for free. Search "design a business logo" and you'll find many options.

Your website plan.
You should have a separate website plan that goes with your business development plan. It should have all the information about your website in it and it should be organic meaning it changes with each update to your website. In the following section, write down the ideas around your website that will eventually be in your final website plan.

Domain name.

You'll need to have several ideas about your domain name because many domain names are already taken. It should be short and memorable and not contain numbers or special characters.

It should also be .COM – that is the most common way known to most people. I know you can get .BIZ or .CA, but stick with .COM, it's just easier for people to remember.

Domain name ideas:

1._____

2._____

3._____

You can check your domain name many places on the web by searching the phrase Domain Name Search.

Final Domain name choice:

_____

For the best search engine results, always register your domain name for three years or longer.

Choose your website hosting company.

Often, you can register your domain name and get a hosting program all in one place . Here are a few of the more popular hosting companies (there are a ton of them out there - these are the ones that I've had experience with):

- Bluehost
- Godaddy
- Amazon Web services
- Network Solutions

Once your domain name is registered and you've chosen your hosting company, you now need to decide what's going to go on your website.

THE GETTING BUSINESS FOR YOUR BUSINESS WORKBOOK

What action do you want your customer to take? Sign up, buy/order, or call/visit? List what your website is for or what you want your customer to do while visiting.

_____

_____

_____

_____

_____

_____

_____

_____

_____

_____

_____

_____

TIP: Visit your competitor's websites and think about what you like about them and don't like and add that to the list below:

_____

_____

THE GETTING BUSINESS FOR YOUR BUSINESS WORKBOOK

List out the sections of your website – this will be the menu that goes across the top of your site.
Most small business websites limit themselves to about 5-6 sections:
- Home (Landing page)
- Product/Service Description
- Portfolio or sample of work
- Event listing
- About
- Contact

For very small business websites, your sections will also be your pages.

Brainstorm the different sections of your website:

_____

_____

_____

_____

_____

_____

_____

_____

_____

_____

_____

_____

_____

_____

_____

_____

Remember when you are thinking about your sections you also need to think about your user/customer experience. How do you want customers to flow through your site? Just an FYI, you have seven seconds to keep a customer on your website until they move onto your competitor.

Describe in detail the perfect user experience when someone comes to your website. What do you want your customer to do/see/learn after seeing your website?

_____

_____

_____

_____

_____

_____

_____

_____

_____

_____

THE GETTING BUSINESS FOR YOUR BUSINESS WORKBOOK

_____

_____

_____

_____

So think about what you just wrote while you are thinking about your final sections.
Final section choices:

1._____

2._____

3._____

4._____

5._____

6._____

7._____

Going forward, if you want to, I find it's very helpful to create a flowchart of a business website because you get to see exactly what your site will look like. You can easily create one in Word or Powerpoint or there are many online flowchart designers (not too many free though).

How are you going to design your website? When you signed up for your hosting plan, you should have been offered a way to design your website. Most sites are designed in:
- Wordpress
- HTML

If you signed up with a all-in-one website company like Wix, Squarespace, or even Bluehost or Network Solutions, you can easily design a small business website. If you decide to design it yourself (which these hosting companies make very easy), just follow the directions or – and don't forget this – you're paying for the help of their customer service so use it!

And if I may say, these days it is really easy to design your website yourself. Having been a professional web designer in the past, I believe that you shouldn't be intimidated by the thought of designing your own website. It's much easier than you think and designing it yourself will give you more control and save you money.

Let's think about your homepage.

- This is where the most important information goes. It's often the first impression a customer will get about your business. So sketch out exactly how your want your website homepage to look. What's the most important information that you want your customers to see first?

HINT: Always put a call-to-action in the upper right-hand corner of your homepage. It works best with white lettering and a red background.

Homepage sketch: Don't forget to include your logo, top menu, upper right-hand corner action item, mid-page content, and footer with menu.

Okay. So now you have your top menu content designed. If you are a larger small business, you will probably want pages under your sections. An example of that would be that if you have an "About" section. Your pages would be "Meet the team", "Testimonials", and "In the news".
To list out your pages, first write the section/menu name and then list the pages underneath.

SECTION_____

PAGES:_____

_____

_____

_____

_____

SECTION_____

PAGES:_____

_____

_____

_____

_____

SECTION_____

PAGES:_____

_____

_____

THE GETTING BUSINESS FOR YOUR BUSINESS WORKBOOK

_____

_____

SECTION_____

 PAGES:_____

_____

_____

_____

_____

SECTION_____

PAGES:_____

_____

_____

_____

_____

SECTION_____

PAGES:_____

_____

_____

_____

SECTION _____

PAGES: _____

_____

_____

_____

_____

Website content.
Videos and images.
If you want your website to open with a video, there are many stock video options available for purchase. Some websites that offer stock video and photography are:
https://pixabay.com/en/
https://www.istockphoto.com/
https://www.fiverr.com
https://www.gettyimages.com

If you are using Wordpress, you can buy a theme that will include free video and image content. Stock photography sites offer images, icons, logos, and videos. Always look at the license about using the work personally or commercially.

Website launch date:
_____

Will you have a blog? It's also good to have a blog plan that's also part of your overall website plan.
List out blog posts ideas and dates:

Blog post idea #1:
Title:
_____

Content ideas:
_____

THE GETTING BUSINESS FOR YOUR BUSINESS WORKBOOK

_____

_____

_____

_____

_____

_____

_____

_____

_____

_____

_____

_____

_____

Blog post #1 launch date:
_____

Blog post idea #2:
Title:
_____

Content ideas:

_____

Blog post #2 launch date:

Blog post idea #3:
Title:
_____

Content ideas:

_____

_____

_____

_____

_____

_____

_____

_____

_____

_____

_____

_____

_____

_____

_____

Blog post #3 launch date:
_____

Blog post idea #4:
Title:
_____

Content ideas:

THE GETTING BUSINESS FOR YOUR BUSINESS WORKBOOK

_____

_____

_____

_____

_____

_____

_____

_____

Blog post #4 launch date:
_____

Your brochure.
There are many different ways of crafting your brochure – easily at home or you can have a graphic designer or professional printer do it for you.
- Tri-fold (most common), Bi-fold (8.5x11 sheet folded and can be printed by you)
- 4 page 11 x 17 (you'll need a printer for this)

It's fine for your brochure to be in black and white so if that's what you can do starting out then do it!
I recently attended the NY Auto show and a large majority of automakers do not offer anything on paper anymore. If you want to save paper and trees (and money), just use your website as your brochure or create your brochure digitally and offer it over social media, email and on your website. But realize that sometimes your customer might like something physical in their hand that they can read so distribution type depends on you and your business.
You can create your brochure in MS Word, Adobe Illustrator (with a free 30-day trial), Canva, or use an online printer like Vistaprint.
What's the purpose of your brochure? Just informational or does it include an order form?

Trifold 8.5 x 11 divided into 3 sections printed front and back:
On the outside will be your front cover, back cover and inside flap. On the front cover you want your most important information, on the contact page all of your contact information and your call-to-action, and on the inside flap you want your benefit bullet points. Make sure that you have the same look and feel as your website.

Tri-fold Brochure Outside

Product/Service Benefits Bulletpoints	Contact Information	Logo Tag line
Inside Flap 3.625" Width	**Back Cover** 3.688" Width	**Front Cover** 3.688" Width

Design the outside of the brochure.

Tri-fold Brochure Inside

The inside of the brochure lays flat when opened up so don't worry about designing across the whole page. You get more design options for designing across the page. I have designed many brochures this way.		
Panel #1 3.688" Width	Panel #2 3.688" Width	Panel #3 3.625" Width

One thing you need to remember when designing anything for print: always make sure you allow for a bleed. A bleed is the area around the edge of your brochure – usually 1/8th inch that you need to leave blank for the printer if you are using photos or graphic elements that touch the edge of the piece. It's so you can get a clean edge on your brochure. If you are outsourcing your printing project, confirm with the printer what their bleed preference is.

Design the inside of the brochure.

You can also design your brochure using an online printer. I have used Vistaprint numerous times and have found them to be a reliable and successful option for a printer. There are many different options for online printers so check the reviews and make a selection.

Outsourcing your brochure:

- A professional graphic designer can run you between $65 & $125+ an hour. A typical brochure project can run anywhere between 5-20+ hours depending on your requirements. When dealing with a graphic designer, make sure you get all the specifications from them before you begin (this will save the graphic designer time and you money) provide your content without typos, your pictures are high resolution (300 pixels-per-inch or PPI), and anything else they request. The more content you provide for the graphic designer, the quicker they will be able to create the design for you and the cheaper it will be. Always make sure that you get the final files from the graphic designer as well as a PDF to use on your website to send to potential clients. Please make sure you have all deadline dates in writing and you negotiate the price for the project before you enter into any contractual relationship with a graphic designer. Also, if you are dealing with a local printer, your graphic designer should be able to work directly with them.
- A local, professional printer. Many printers also provide graphic design services. The printers that I have dealt with charge $125 an hour for those services. It's an easy option because they will design and print your brochure and you get to use a local business! (That's always good).

If you are outsourcing your brochure, make sure you know the requirements for the file like image resolution, Pantone color, and size requirements. Also, you are responsible for any typos in your brochure that need to be corrected. <u>The printer is not responsible for typos or grammatical errors.</u>

Email newsletters.

Small business owners often produce both hard copy and email newsletters for their customers.

A hard copy printed or PDF newsletter is easy to produce in any of the publishing programs listed in the previous section and can be printed and snail-mailed or emailed directly to your customer list as a PDF. Many small business owners find success doing a digital newsletter and it is a cost effective strategy for those just starting out.

An email newsletter is also an easy way to engage with potential customers. Always make your newsletter a similar design to your website/brochure or any other marketing communications that you are using. Same colors, font, and similar images help build your brand. Consistency is key!

There are many options for email newsletter programs and designs on the internet. Two that I'm familiar with are:

>Constant Contact

>MailChimp

Email newsletter templates.

>Most email newsletters are cut into four sections.

- Top
- Mid-top
- Center
- Bottom

The top is where your logo or business name goes. It's also where – if you are sending a unsolicited email to a list – you insert the term "Advertisement" or "Solicitation" above your logo.

> **For more information on unsolicited business email rules, search for the CAN SPAM Act of 2003.**

The mid-top is where you might put a graphic or text describing what your newsletter is about.

The center is where your written or other image content goes.

The bottom is your call-to-action, contact information, and social media links.

Also, you get an opportunity to add a subject line and a headline. Please add some keywords when writing these because they also have an SEO component to them.

Email newsletter design is an art and a science. You can use as many images as you like and most people keep their newsletters very simple. To me, it's really a way for your product or service to stay in the front of your customer's mind.

Just search "best email newsletters" and you will get a slew of examples.

Best time to send your email newsletters? Lot's of research on this topic has been done and Tuesdays and Thursdays are two of the best days. The best times are before 8am or after 11am.

What should you write about?

- Grand opening
- New product or service offerings
- Client testimonials
- A how-to instructional post
- How your product or service helps people
- A customer success story
- Upcoming events where your customers can meet you
- Promotions/coupons
- An online survey of your P/S with a giveaway of a $25 Amazon gift card
- New talent acquisitions

Want people to sign up for your newsletter from your website?

Both Constant Contact and MailChimp offer a way to do that – it's really easy to set up. And how do you get people to sign up? Offer something for free. Can you offer a recipe, or video, or something that will make their life better?

What *"Free"* thing can you offer your customer in exchange for their email/name/address/phone that totally benefits their life, makes them feel good about you, and turns them into a customer, friend, or partner?

_____

_____

_____

_____

_____

_____

THE GETTING BUSINESS FOR YOUR BUSINESS WORKBOOK

List out newsletter ideas and dates:
Newsletter idea #1:
Title:

_____

Content ideas:

_____

_____

_____

_____

_____

_____

_____

_____

_____

_____

_____

Newsletter #1 send date:

_____

Newsletter idea #2:
Title:

___

Content ideas:

___

___

___

___

___

___

___

___

___

___

___

___

Newsletter #2 send date:

___

Newsletter idea #3:
Title:

_____

Content ideas:

_____

_____

_____

_____

_____

_____

_____

_____

_____

_____

_____

_____

Newsletter #3 send date:

_____

Your newsletter doesn't always have to be about business! Remember, reading your newsletter should bring something to the reader's party, or else you'll end up in the spam bin or the unthinkable: unsubscribed!

Always include a way to buy your service or product in your newsletter or any customer email. Ask for the sale!!!

Landing pages/strategy: A landing page is a specific page on your website dedicated to a link attached to your email newsletter (or digital banner). Use a landing page in conjunction with a link in your newsletter with a promotion. Mailchimp has such a service or you can design one yourself in Wordpress or whatever program used to design your site. Remember, as with your website, your landing page should have a similar look and feel and always put the call-to-action you want most – a donation, purchase, call – in red or some other contrasting color up in the right-hand corner.

THE GETTING BUSINESS FOR YOUR BUSINESS WORKBOOK

Sketch out a newsletter design.

There are many other ways to design your newsletter, but if you are just starting out, I believe keeping it simple is the best thing.

Chapter 6

WHAT'S NEXT?

There, you did it. You wrote and designed a plan for your business.
What's next? ACTION. Through action and courage you will be successful.
First, remember why you are doing this. List your top five reasons for wanting to become an entrepreneur.

1._____

2._____

3._____

4._____

5._____

Business projected opening date: (When are you going to start selling your product or service?)

_____

Take what you have written and the dates you have decided upon and get a daily, weekly, and monthly calendar. This will allow you to see the dates and goals that you have written down and decide what the actions are that need to be accomplished to reach those goals.
**And then, just start. Just start doing your thing and don't worry about the "how" and the "what", it will all happen. Don't worry about the outcome and just keep moving forward because it's the

actions that equal results.

If you would like a more in-depth look at any of these topics including social media, tradeshows, and CRM development, please download or order my accompanying book *Getting Business for Your Business | Do-It-Yourself Strategies to Increase Your Small Business' Bottom Line.*

And if this book has helped you , if you would be so kind and leave me a good review on Amazon, I would appreciate it.

Thank you. Now go forth and make money!

Below find the one, two, and four year goal update sections where you can record any changes that you want to make for the future.

One year goal update:

Revised profit estimate:
_____

If you have a product, how will you make that product? Will you hold inventory or does someone else do that?
_____
_____
_____
_____
_____
_____
_____
_____

Who are your suppliers?
_____
_____
_____

If you have a service, how will you implement that service?
_____
_____
_____
_____
_____
_____
_____
_____

How will you promote that service? (Social Media, tradeshows, word-of-mouth, advertising, etc.? List a few ideas.)
_____
_____
_____
_____

THE GETTING BUSINESS FOR YOUR BUSINESS WORKBOOK

_____

_____

_____

_____

_____

How many customers do you want to have?
_____

How many long-term relationships will you develop? These can be with suppliers or other business colleagues as well as customers.
_____

List some ideas on where you might meet customers:
(tradeshows, networking)
_____

_____

_____

_____

_____

_____

_____

_____

_____

What major expenses will you have? Where are you getting the money to pay them?

_____

_____

_____

Thoughts on your sales strategy? (low price, technological, what makes you different?)

_____

_____

_____

_____

_____

_____

_____

_____

How will you promote your product? Advertising/Social Media/website/tradeshows/home parties?

_____

_____

_____

Changes or updates to my product, service, or customer service strategy that I want to make:

___

___

___

___

___

___

___

Two year goal update:
Revised profit estimate:
___

If you have a product, how will you make that product? Will you hold inventory or does someone else do that?
___

___

___

___

Who are your suppliers?
___

___

___

THE GETTING BUSINESS FOR YOUR BUSINESS WORKBOOK

If you have a service, how will you implement that service?

_____

_____

_____

_____

_____

_____

How will you promote that service? (Social Media, Tradeshows, Word-of-mouth, Advertising, etc? List a few ideas.)

_____

_____

_____

_____

_____

_____

How many customers do you want to have?

_____

_____

How many long-term relationships will you develop? These can be with suppliers or other business colleagues as well as customers.

_____

List some ideas on where you might meet new customers: tradeshows, networking

_____

_____

_____

_____

_____

What major expenses will you have? Where are you getting the money to pay them?

_____

_____

_____

_____

_____

_____

_____

Thoughts on a new sales strategy? (low price, technological, what can you improve?)

THE GETTING BUSINESS FOR YOUR BUSINESS WORKBOOK

_____

_____

_____

_____

_____

_____

_____

_____

_____

_____

_____

_____

New ways you will promote your product? Advertising/Social Media/website/tradeshows/home parties?

_____

_____

_____

_____

_____

_____

_____

_____

Changes or updates to my product, service, or customer service strategy that I want to make:

_____

_____

_____

_____

_____

_____

_____

Four year goal update:
Revised profit estimate:

_____

If you have a product, how will you make that product? Will you hold inventory or does someone else do that?

_____

THE GETTING BUSINESS FOR YOUR BUSINESS WORKBOOK

_____

_____

_____

Who are your suppliers?

_____

_____

New service implementations:

_____

_____

_____

_____

_____

_____

New ways to promote your service or product? (Social Media, tradeshows, word-of-mouth, advertising, etc.? List a few ideas.)

_____

_____

_____

_____

How many new customers do you want to have?

How many long-term relationships will you develop? These can be with suppliers or other business colleagues as well as customers.

List some new ideas on where you might meet customers: (tradeshows, networking, new email newsletter?)

What major expenses will you have? Where are you getting the money to pay them?

Thoughts on your sales strategy? (low price, technological, what makes you different?)

THE GETTING BUSINESS FOR YOUR BUSINESS WORKBOOK

_____

_____

_____

_____

_____

_____

New ways you will promote your product or service?
Advertising/Social Media/website/tradeshows/home parties?

_____

_____

_____

_____

_____

_____

_____

Changes or updates to my product, service, or customer service strategy that I want to make:

_____

_____

Notes:

THE GETTING BUSINESS FOR YOUR BUSINESS WORKBOOK

Appendix A Resources for starting a business from the Small Business Administration

The Small Business Administration is a great resource for any small business related topic. I encourage you to scour their website to get the latest information for helping your small business succeed. Http://www.SBA.Gov

How to write a business plan: https://www.sba.gov/business-guide/plan-your-business/write-your-business-plan

How to choose and claim your business name: https://www.sba.gov/blogs/how-choose-claim-and-protect-your-business-name-online-and-offline

Register your business: https://www.sba.gov/blogs/how-register-your-small-business-four-steps

Sole Proprietorship or LLC? Tips for choosing your business structure: https://www.sba.gov/business-guide/launch-your-business/choose-business-structure

What the deal with taxes on your small business? https://www.sba.gov/business-guide/manage-your-business/pay-taxes?utm_medium=email&utm_source=govdelivery

How to patent your product: https://www.uspto.gov/patents-getting-started/general-information-concerning-patents

Appendix B Business Development Overview: Strategy Based Around a Product
The Plate Lighter

Product Description: A portable, solar and optional battery-powered ceramic plate heater with an adjustable light that clamps onto a plate and prevents your home/outdoor cooked meal from getting cold while you are:

- Waiting for everyone to come to the table
- Camping
- Waiting for other food to finish cooking
- Just sitting and eating
- Waiting for the power to come back on

Competitors:

- Portable plate warmers
- Nothing similar on the market

Domain name:

- Platelighter.com

Price point: $12.99

Distribution channel:

- Present:
    - Website
    - Small, local tradeshows
    - Investigate Amazon and Ebay
- Future:
    - Large camping retailers
    - Large home retailers

Marketing Strategy:

The problem that the Plate Lighter solves is it prevents you having to eat cold food when you are camping (or the fire goes out, or you're waiting for your family to come home/arrive at table)

Features:

- 2 light selections:
    - Firelight
    - Straight LED
- Warms the plate but never burns your hand
- Safe to the touch
- Long lasting charge from solar or rechargeable battery
- Ceramic heater never overcooks food

Benefits:

- Always serve hot food to your family
- Never lose all that hard work of cooking dinner
- Environmentally friendly
- Gives you the freedom of cooking good home made meals even while camping and RV'ing
- See your food even if the power goes out
- Easy on the eyes with two light settings

- Slow eater? Keeps your food warm even if you are on the "Get up from the table" diet

Basic messaging:

- Do you home cook only to have your food get cold while waiting for your family to come to the table?
- For just $12.99 you get four plate warmers that keep your food like it just came out of the oven.
- You'll never burn your hands with our patented ceramic heat source. Even if a child grabs it, it will never burn any skin.
- Easy to remove – slides right off your plate and can even go in the dishwasher!
- Great for camping with a light on your food (even if your power goes out, you'll always be able see what you are eating).

Marketing communications/promotion strategy:

- Design Logo in MS Word (It can be done!) or online designer (Canva)
- Design and order business cards on Vista print
- Brochure:
    - Designed at home with printer and your own pictures (or images from Pixabay) of:
        - Camping
        - Eating your great home cooked meal with friends
        - Happy people eating
        - The product itself and an illustration of how it works
        - Include benefits to the customer
    - Brochure to be left at campsites (leave a few of the Plate Lighters with the campground managers)
        - Create content including videos and images
- Website:
    - After signing up for hosting and domain name, use an easy Wordpress template to design website – or have Hosting company design e-commerce site.
    - Include blog with recipes
    - Sign up for Paypal to accept payments

AND/OR

Develop Plate Lighter Social Media presence

  o Create Facebook page to be your website

- - Create posts that act like a blog
    - Create a group about camping recipes
  - Create a Podcast about cooking while camping
  - Create Twitter account - @platelighter
    - Tweet your recipes, product usage ideas, product updates, images of customers, or product benefits

Email newsletter:

- Sign up for Constant Contact or MailChimp
- Reach out to all friends/colleagues on Facebook, email, text, Twitter, Linkedin and request they sign up!
- Send one newsletter a month filled with recipes, product images, and ways to use the Plate Lighter.

Tradeshows:

Research local tradeshows

- Be where campers are
- 4h fairs/Boat Shows
- Visit RV shows and talk to RV manufacturers about having Plate Lighter packaged with RVs
- Visit/call those tradeshows and research the different attendee

ABOUT THE AUTHOR

L.A. Dyer has been in corporate communications for over 30 years writing and designing for both Fortune 500 companies as well as small and start-up organizations. Visit http://www.LADyerbooks.com for more exciting products from this author.

www.ingramcontent.com/pod-product-compliance
Lightning Source LLC
Chambersburg PA
CBHW071039240526
45469CB00006BD/2261